THE WEAT ERMEN OF BEN NEVIS

1883-1904

Marjory Roy

First published 2004
ISBN 0 948090 24 3

ACKNOWLEDGEMENTS

The original data, observation sheets and log books from the Ben Nevis and Fort William Observatories are kept in the archives of the Edinburgh Meteorological Office, which contain the meteorological records for Scotland. The author would like to thank the staff of that office for their interest and help in preparing this book. Parts of the text are based on an article by James Paton, first published in 1954, and reprinted in booklet form by the Royal Meteorological Society in 1983 to mark the centenary of the opening of the Observatory.

Modern photographs of Ben Nevis and of the Observatory ruins have been provided by Alex Gillespie of Fort William.

The photographs of William Speirs Bruce and of Omond House in the South Orkneys were provided by the Royal Scottish Geographical Society.

Printed in Fort William by Nevisprint Ltd www.nevisprint.co.uk

Published by The Royal Meteorological Society

Contents

ROYAL METEOROLOGICAL SOCIETY

Introduction

"Land of the mountain and the flood" was how Sir Walter Scott described Scotland and many, inhabitant and visitor alike, would agree with this description. But there is much more to Scotland's climate than an abundance of rain, and indeed, despite popular belief, not all of the country is exceptionally wet. Although of modest height when compared with the Rockies, the Alps or the Himalayas, the mountains of Scotland have a very strong effect on its weather, often giving rise to marked contrasts in rainfall and cloud cover between west and east or north and south. On the mountains themselves there can be rapid changes with height of temperature, humidity and windspeed, changes which can have life-threatening consequences for unwary hillwalkers.

In comparison with low-ground sites, there have been very few observations on the mountains of Scotland, largely because of the remoteness of the sites from human habitation and the difficulties involved in using standard observing instruments, which rapidly become iced-up and useless. One notable exception, which is sometimes forgotten by those who lament the lack of data, is provided by Britain's only mountain observatory, which operated on the summit of Ben Nevis from 1883 to 1904. The story of the setting up and running of this Observatory is a fascinating one, which is well-worth retelling, and the data obtained from there and from the automatic weather stations which have been set up more recently on Cairngorm, Aonach Mor and the Cairnwell, can be used to give a better understanding of weather conditions on and among the mountains of Scotland.

Ben Nevis and its Observatory

Although Ben Nevis rises directly from sea-level, it is actually about 50 km from the west coast of mainland Scotland. This is because Loch Linnhe, at the head of which it lies, is a very long sea loch, which runs inland in a southwesterly-northeasterly direction from the Sound of Mull.

Seen from Corpach, on the opposite side of Loch Linnhe from Fort William, Ben Nevis appears as a large bulk of a mountain, with Meall an t'Suidhe in the foreground, but the actual summit area is a relatively narrow plateau, lying east-west, with great cliffs to the north and steep slopes to the south down into Glen Nevis. As the observers eventually discovered, the local topography affects dramatically the winds that are observed on the slopes and at the summit of the mountain.

The ascent of Ben Nevis, the highest mountain in Britain, is a major objective of many summer visitors to Lochaber and those who accomplish it may wonder at the existence of the broad "pony track", with its gradient of not more than one in five. Then, when they finally reach the summit, they find the ruins of a substantial building, with an emergency shelter perched on the remains of its tower. Someone may tell them that these are the ruins of an observatory, but, if

ial view of Ben Nevis and Carn Mor Dearg from the southeast.

Ben Nevis from Corpach.

they are experiencing the all too frequent hill fog, they must wonder at the advisability of erecting an astronomical observatory at such a cloudy location. The clue to the true function of the building may be found (if the last of the winter snow is not covering it) from a plaque which was placed on the foundations in 1969.

These are the remains of the
METEOROLOGICAL OBSERVATORY
which, with the path from Achintee, was built in 1883
with publicly subscribed funds. It was managed by the
SCOTTISH METEOROLOGICAL SOCIETY
and representatives of the
ROYAL SOCIETIES OF LONDON & EDINBURGH.
and representatives of the
ROYAL SOCIETIES OF LONDON & EDINBURGH.
Hourly observations were maintained for 21 years
and sent by telegraph via Fort William to
meteorological services throughout Europe.
The Brocken Spectre seen from here on cloud in the
Great Corrie by C T R Wilson in 1894 led him to
researches which culminated in the development
of the Wilson Cloud Chamber, and for which he was
awarded a Nobel Prize in 1927.

It was an enthusiastic band of Scottish meteorologists who conceived the idea of building this, the only British mountain observatory, and who finally achieved all their aims, except that of persuading the State to take over their fully equipped observatory and mountain laboratory. Their original aim was not to record mountain weather (in the early 1880's the pleasures and dangers of winter climbing in Scotland had still to be discovered), but to investigate the vertical structure of the lower part of the atmosphere and so improve weather forecasting. After the Observatory closed in 1904 many years were to pass before regular weather observations were again made on the summit of one of Scotland's inhospitable mountains, this time by Heriot-Watt University's automatic weather station, which was installed on the summit of Cairngorm in 1977.

Proposal for a mountain observatory in Scotland

Before the invention of radio, measurements of the vertical structure of the atmosphere could only be obtained from occasional manned balloon flights or from instruments carried on kites or captive balloons and subsequently retrieved at ground level. It was realised that the only way to obtain regular observations at higher levels would be to set up manned mountain observatories and by about 1875 these were being established in the United States, Mexico, India, France, Italy, Switzerland, Austria, Germany and Russia.

It is perhaps not generally realised that from the time of its foundation in 1855 until 1920, (when the Meteorological Office took over this responsibility) it was the Scottish Meteorological Society which maintained a network of climatological stations in Scotland and collected and analysed their statistics. The observers were unpaid and the report of the Council of the Society for 1875 contrasted this with the state of affairs in America whose "weather stations are managed by government officials at public expense". The mountain observatories at Mount Washington (1916 metres) and Pike's Peak (4314 metres) were cited.

At this time the Meteorological Office in London, under the supervision of the Meteorological Council, financed, from its annual grant of £15,000, the running of 7 Observatories (Kew, Valentia, Armagh, Falmouth, Stonyhurst, Glasgow and Aberdeen) at which automatic recordings of pressure, temperature (dry and wet bulb), rainfall and wind were made. On a daily basis the Meteorological Office also received weather observations by telegraph from a network of sites across the British Isles and Europe and these were used to prepare a daily weather report, which included the observations, a map of the surface pressure and temperature distribution at 0800 and forecasts for the next 24 hours for 11 areas within the British Isles. Warnings of impending storms were sent to coastal stations.

In 1877 Mr Milne Home, Chairman of the Council of the Scottish Meteorological Society, pointed out the advantage of Ben Nevis as a high-level station and in 1878 he reported to the Council that "he had ascended Ben Nevis with the view of ascertaining the practicability of establishing a station on the top of that mountain and had also made enquiries from the proprietors and the local

5

David Milne Home.

parties for that same object, with the result that the proposal was quite practical, provided funds were forthcoming to meet the expense of the building and pay the observers." (Since he was aged 73 at the time and there was no path to the top, his climb showed a considerable commitment to the cause).

Accordingly the cost of establishing mountain observatories in other countries was ascertained; the Honorary Secretary, Mr Thomas Stevenson – lighthouse engineer, designer of the thermometer screen and father of Robert Louis Stevenson – prepared plans; and it was estimated that "a sum of £1,000 would be required to build and £300 annually to uphold Ben Nevis Observatory", for, while their observers were not normally paid "apparently feeling pleased and honoured by the trust reposed in them", the mountain observer "has to be compensated for being excluded from any profitable occupation on his own account".

As Mr Milne Home was later to describe at the Banquet held in the Town Hall at Fort William to celebrate the opening of the Observatory, representatives of the Society then "proceeded to London, and had interviews with the Chancellor of the Exchequer, the Secretary of the Treasury, the Government Grant Committee, and the Meteorological Council, which had at its disposal a Parliamentary grant of £15,000 a year. But he was sorry to say that a whole year was wasted, each department referring them in most polite terms to the other as more likely to help. The only promise they could get was from the Meteorological Council, which stated that if the observatory was erected, it would give £100 a year towards its expenses". A condition of this offer was that a copy of the record of observations would be supplied to the Meteorological Office. Encouraged by substantial offers of help from many Scottish firms and individuals, the Council resolved to proceed with preliminary arrangements and it was recorded that "there was every probability that the Government, if properly appealed to and being shown that the Scottish public had undertaken to erect and equip a proper observatory, could scarcely refuse to take the requisite steps for its proper maintenance". That this hope was a vain one was later to become only too evident.

Clement Wragge

There now came upon the scene a remarkable personality. On learning of the Society's plans for Ben Nevis, a Mr Clement Wragge wrote to the Secretary offering to climb the Ben daily during the summer of 1881 to make observations. The offer was accepted and from 1 June until 14 October simultaneous observations were made on the summit and at Fort William. A small stone hut and protecting cairn for the barometer and a cage for the thermometers were erected on the summit to the plan of Stevenson and thither Wragge climbed each day. (The supporting structure for the thermometer cage can still be seen beside the ruins of the Observatory). He did not ascend by the route that was to be chosen for the bridle path but, starting from near the Ben Nevis distillery on the road to Inverness, he went on horseback up an existing track on the north side of Meall an t'Suidhe

Clement Wragge.

(hill of rest) to its lochan and thence on foot direct to the summit plateau, following the course of the Red Burn. He eventually set himself a rigorous programme of observation to which he stuck religiously: Sea-Level 4.40 a.m.; Lochan Meall an t'Suidhe (half-way) 6.30; Spring at 3,375 ft (1029 metres) 8.15; Summit 9, 9.30 and 10; Spring 10.50; Lochan 1 p.m.; and Sea-Level 3.30. Simultaneously Mrs Wragge made observations near sea-level at Fort William. Day by day, despite blizzard, gale and pouring rain and often laden with a thick coating of rime or glaze, Wragge – the "inclement rag" was his inevitable nickname – and his Newfoundland dog, Renzo, struggled on to the summit plateau at the appointed time. Frequently on reaching the summit he could not manipulate the key that opened the door of the instrument cage until he had made a fire to thaw his benumbed fingers.

Ben Nevis
Meteorological Observatory
— First Established May 31st 1881 —

under the Auspices of the Scottish Meteor'l Society

Clemt L Wragge, F.R.G.S, F.M.S

Observer & Superintendent

Lat 56° 47' N   Long 5° 0' W

Height above Mean Sea Level

	Feet
Barometer	4406?
Dry-bulb	4408?
Rim of rain gauge	4404?

"Rough" Observation-book

[For Instruments in use, Notes and Explanations see Appendix]

B: Nº I

(June 1st to 7th inclusive 1881)

Title page of Wragge's observation book 1881.

At a meeting of the Society on 22 March 1882 a gold medal was presented to Wragge in token of "his great skill in organising this work, his fertility of resource in emergencies, his indefatigable energy and his undaunted devotion to his work". His observation books are held in the archives of the Edinburgh Meteorological Office and their style is fully in keeping with his flamboyant and energetic character. Wragge continued his observations during the summer of 1882, with the help of two assistants (one of whom was Angus Rankin, who joined the Observatory staff in October 1883) and increased the number of his intermediate stations to six. The two assistants continued the observations, though with fewer intermediate stations, through the summer of 1883.

The conditions that they had to endure, even in the middle of summer, can be appreciated from some of the notes in the observation books. For example on 19 July 1882 Wragge recorded in the margin "Barometer pumping; hands so swollen owing to the wet that I couldn't reset it to ascertain to what extent precisely it pumped. I had indeed the greatest difficulty in turning the vernier screw this morning, having sometimes to use both hands, right hand being almost useless. Such is the effect of wet and cold upon the flesh". The temperature on the summit that day was around 3°C, with intermittent slight rain, hill fog making everything saturated with moisture, and a gusty southwesterly wind.

On 26 June 1883 (just after midsummer) conditions were even more extreme for Angus Rankin. Rain had fallen continuously since 2 a.m. and by the time that he reached the Lochan at half-way at 6 a.m. it was falling heavily. When he emerged onto the summit plateau (called by the observers the "Plateau of Storms") "the wind began to blow with force 10. I had three times to lie down and take hold of stones till the squall was past". Reaching the summit at 8 a.m. he recorded that the wind was force 9 to 10 from the east, rain was "falling in sheets" and the wind was "lifting old snow, in large pieces, from edge of precipice and carrying it across". He sensibly "would not venture to gauge C which is situated at edge of precipice". The temperature was around 5°C, and the relative humidity was 100%. During the two hours that he remained at the summit, presumably spending much of the time in the shelter hut, the wind blew at around force 8 to 10 from the east, rain continued to fall, though not as heavily as at 8 a.m., and patches of cloud drifted across the summit. Things were little better on the return journey until he reached the Lochan and at the "Plateau of Storms" he reported "The wind was roaring in the Corries, and sweeping past at a force of 10 to 11. Here it began raining very heavily."

Meanwhile down in Fort William a strong northeasterly wind had been blowing all day down the Great Glen but just before he reached there at about

Achintore Road, Fort William, late 19th century.

2 p.m. the wind changed to south-southwesterly and fell light.

The weather data, which the Meteorological Office in London received from the telegraph stations in the British Isles and Europe, were normally recorded at 0800 and 1800 GMT. These data included the pressure in inches of mercury (reduced to mean sea-level), dry and wet bulb temperatures in degrees Fahrenheit, wind force (on the Beaufort scale) and wind direction. The current weather was indicated in the form of Beaufort letters. (Wet bulb temperatures were not given for the 1800 observation). The dew point (the temperature to which air must be cooled for condensation to occur) is a useful measure of the humidity of the air and can be calculated from the dry and wet bulb temperatures. These data have been converted to the units normally used now on meteorological charts – pressure in millibars, temperature in degrees Celsius, wind speed in knots (nautical miles per hour) – and plotted on the charts using the format shown below. The concept of weather fronts was only introduced in 1918, by the Norwegian J Bjerknes, so fronts did not appear on the original maps.

PLOTTED DATA ON WEATHER MAPS

air temperature (dry bulb)   surface pressure in millibars

wind speed and direction ⟶

dew point

WIND SPEED SYMBOLS

| 5 knots (force 2) | 10 knots (force 3) | 15 knots (force 4) | 20 knots (force 5) | 25 knots (force6) | 30 knots (force 7) | 35 knots (force 8) (gale force) | 40 knots (force 9) |

(1 knot = 1.125 miles per hour or 1.854 km per hour)

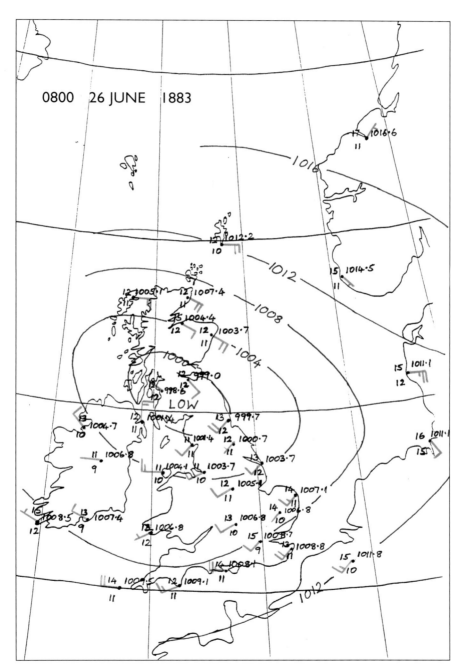

0800　26 JUNE　1883

In the Northern Hemisphere winds circulate in an anticlockwise direction around depressions (Buys Ballot's Law) and the weather situation on 26 June 1883 can be illustrated by the observations from telegraph stations over the UK, which were sent to the Meteorological Office in London. The weather map on page 11 shows the surface pressure field and the observed wind speeds and directions at 8 a.m. on 26 June. A depression, which had formed over northeastern France on 25th June, had deepened as it moved northwestwards across England and Scotland on the 26th. To the north of the depression the pressure pattern indicated that, away from the immediate effect of the local topography, winds above the mountains would have been easterly, but the northeasterlies observed at Fort William were clearly due to funnelling along the Great Glen.

One of the features of the summit weather, which stands out in the observations, was the gustiness of the wind, especially when it came from a northerly direction, over the great cliffs. Although it was not appreciated at the time the local topography had a major effect on the observed winds, with "free air" northwesterlies above the mountain being changed into very gusty winds of variable, mainly northerly direction at the summit.

Naturally Wragge's Ben Nevis exploits enjoyed considerable publicity. A Times correspondent ascended with him on a day of fearful weather and a startling article, occupying no less than three columns, ensued. His work served the important purpose of directing the attention of the whole country to the Society's project. The weather conditions experienced by Wragge and his assistants had shown that the automatic recording instruments used in the observatories of the period would be quite useless in the severe conditions at the top of the mountain and that manual observations would have to be made throughout the 24 hours, requiring more observers than had originally been envisaged. It was also obvious that the building would have to be able to withstand winds that were well beyond any that had been experienced on lower ground.

At a general meeting, Sir William Thomson, later Lord Kelvin, proposed "that this meeting, in view of the great importance of high-level stations and the value of the results shown to have been already obtained during the last year on Ben Nevis from Mr Wragge's observations, recommend the Council at once to appeal to the British public for funds wherewith to erect on Ben Nevis a permanent observatory". So, early in 1883, the appeal was launched and in a few months a sum of over £4,000 was subscribed in amounts ranging from a bawbee to £200. Her Majesty, Queen Victoria, headed the subscription list with a donation of £50.

The Directors of the Observatory were the members of the Council of the Scottish Meteorological Society and representatives of the Royal Societies of

London and Edinburgh. Since Mrs Cameron Campbell was the entailed proprietor of the estate of Callart which included the summit of Ben Nevis, legal difficulties arose concerning her powers to grant a conveyance for the land required. This was solved by the insertion of a special clause in an Entail Bill then passing through Parliament. As a result she was able to grant a feu of one acre on the summit of Ben Nevis in favour of Council of the Royal Society of Edinburgh, which, being incorporated by Royal Charter, was entitled to hold heritable property for scientific purposes.

Minutes of the first meeting of the Directors of the Ben Nevis observatory.

Route marker posts across the "plateau of storms".

The Construction of the Bridle Path
and the Observatory

With the necessary funds secured, the summer of 1883 was one of feverish activity on the mountain. The Council proceeded at once to arrange for the construction of a bridle path along the route suggested by the local schoolmaster, from the farm of Achintee in lovely Glen Nevis, along the southwestern flanks of Meall an t-Suidhe, up to the Lochan and thence by long zig-zags up the western shoulder of the Ben to the summit plateau. Nowhere did the gradient of the 2 metres wide and 8 km long track exceed one in five and there were a number of gullies and streams to be bridged on the lower part of the route. The price of £798 seems scant reward for such remarkable labours.

The road had to be completed before building material could be carried up, but meanwhile local masons were dressing granite blocks on and near the summit, since the stone work of the Observatory was to be built from the mountain itself. The architect was Mr Sydney Mitchell, the son of one of the

Route of the pony track up Ben Nevis.

founder members of the Scottish Meteorological Society, Sir Arthur Mitchell. The original structure consisted of one room, about 4 metres square, from which three small sleeping bunks were entered. There were also store rooms and a coal cellar. At their base the walls were about 3½ metres thick and the interior had a double lining of wood covered with felt. The lead covered roof was overlaid

Minutes recording the appointment of R T Omond as the Superintendent.

with snow boarding. The building operations were of necessity constructed at great speed, since all had to be completed and provisions brought in for the winter before snow closed the road. It was intended that the Observatory would be extended the following summer. A heavily armoured telegraph cable was laid from Fort William to the Observatory to provide communication to the outside world.

Meanwhile the Directors had to deal with the important matter of the appointment of the first Superintendent. On 23 July 1883 Clement Wragge wrote to the Directors offering himself as a candidate and a letter from Mr R T Omond was received at the same time. After some discussion it was resolved that the post should be advertised in the "Scotsman" and "Glasgow Herald" newspapers and in the scientific periodical "Nature". Nineteen applications were received for the post and eventually Robert Traill Omond was unanimously elected at a meeting of the Directors. Clement Wragge went off in a huff to Australia, where he established the Weather Bureau at Brisbane and Mountain Observatories on Mount Wellington and Mont Koshiusko. The decision not to give him the post must have appeared to him an unjust response to all his labours, but a less flamboyant character was clearly needed for the cramped conditions and routine work of the new Observatory. Omond had already shown his scientific expertise while working with Professor Tait in the Department of Natural Philosophy at Edinburgh University and he proved to be an able Superintendent. His two assistants were Angus Rankin and J Duncan. Duncan resigned in April 1884 and was replaced by J Miller, who served on the Observatory staff for the rest of the period of operation.

On 17 October 1883, little more than five months after the commencement of building operations, the Observatory was formally opened by Mrs Cameron Campbell, on a day which gave the 100 or so participants in the ceremony an appropriate introduction to the conditions likely to be experienced by the observers. According to the report in the "Scotsman" newspaper of 18 October 1883: "at seven o'clock that morning the rain was descending in torrents. The tops of the surrounding hills were seen through the steamy-looking clouds by which they were enveloped to be covered in snow... Fortunately, about eight o'clock a marvellous change occurred. The rain suddenly ceased, and the sun breaking through the clouds gave promise of a brighter day. Hope rose with the barometer, and though the weather afterwards was not all that might have been desired, it was wonderfully good for the season". Nine of the ladies in the party, including Mrs Cameron Campbell, were mounted on ponies and two other ladies walked to summit. The snow-line was reached at about 700 metres and the snow

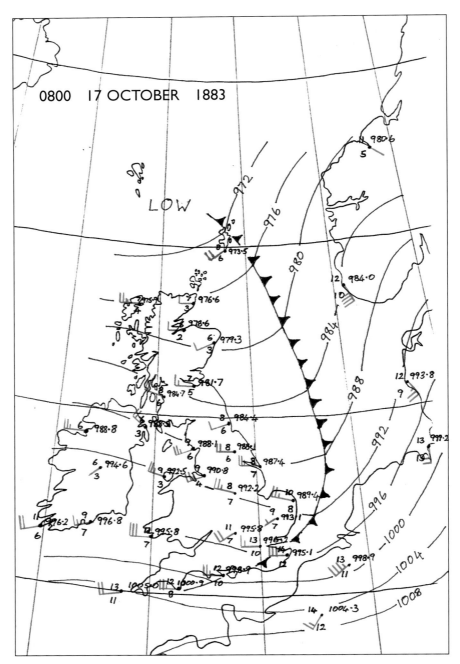

0800 17 OCTOBER 1883

on the path gradually increased until it reached a depth of about 30 cm. The welcoming party included the architect, Mr Sydney Mitchell, who presented Mrs Cameron Campbell with the key to the door, which she unlocked, and as many as possible crowded gratefully in out of the wind. After the Observatory had been formally declared open at a ceremony inside the building the party emerged to find that a storm was raging, with blinding clouds of drift and hailstorms.

Daily weather maps based on the telegraph stations' observations show that on 15 October 1883 there was a temporary ridge of high pressure over the British Isles, but that the barograph was falling very rapidly to the southwest of Ireland, heralding the approach of a depression which moved northeast across the Western Isles of Scotland on the 16th. By the morning of 17 October the centre lay to the north of Scotland with the isobars indicating a showery west-northwesterly airstream over Fort William area. William Whyte had made the routine daily ascent and reported, at around 9 a.m., a summit temperature of -2.4°C and a fresh, gusty northeasterly wind, in contrast to the light to moderate southwesterlies observed at Fort William. (The next day he was unable to reach the top, due to continuous, blinding, heavy hail, which made his clothes a frozen mass).

That evening a banquet was held in the Town Hall of Fort William. After paying tribute to the generosity of subscribers from both Scotland and England Mr Milne Home said that "he was glad they had not received half from the Government, because it was most probable the Government would have imposed conditions which might have interfered with their Scottish management of the institution, and he for one was in favour of local Scottish management for local affairs".

PLAN

of the

BEN NEVIS OBSERVATORY.

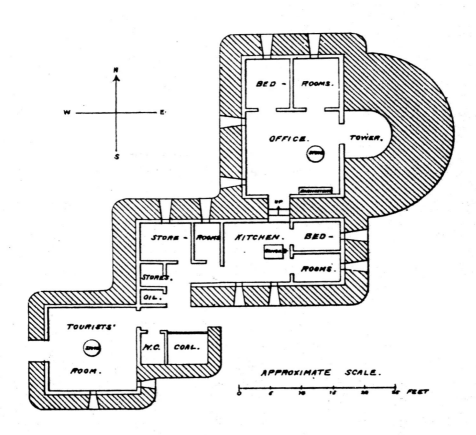

APPROXIMATE SCALE.

Observational, Instrumental and Other Difficulties

By the end of October Mr Omond and his assistants were in residence and they made the final preparations for the start of hourly observations, which commenced on 28 November 1883. The first winter turned out to be one of the stormiest experienced at the Observatory and because no arrangement had been made for keeping the doorway clear of snow, a great deal of digging was required. Once snow began to lie to a depth of a foot or so on the mountain, strong winds caused drifts to accumulate round, and eventually to submerge the building. A passage was dug outwards and upwards from the door, but as soon as the wind rose it was constantly filled up with snow. That winter the tunnel grew to over 10 metres in length with a rise in level of 4 metres to the outside snow surface. All attempts to keep the doorway clear in bad weather were hopeless and as a result observations during the first winter were frequently interrupted.

The inconvenience to the observers of performing the office, laboratory and telegraph work as well as cooking, eating and washing within the confines of one small room can well be imagined. During the summer of 1884 considerable extensions and improvements to the building were made. They comprised another room slightly larger than the first, for use as an office and laboratory, two

Observatory in winter.   Observatory in summer.

21

additional bedrooms, an extra room for visitors to the Observatory, and a 10 metre high wooden tower, on which anemometers to measure the wind speed and direction were mounted. The tower provided an upper exit door onto the roof in winter when the main door was blocked with snow and also, having windows all round, served as an outlook. The wooden framework for the tower had first been fitted and erected in Edinburgh, then dismantled and transported to Fort William.

It was seldom that the Observatory horses carrying stores in panniers could make the ascent between about the middle of November and the end of May, so provisions to last nine months had to be kept in store.

With the tower in operation it was possible to maintain an hourly routine of weather observations throughout the twenty-four hours, except during exceptionally stormy periods such as occurred on 21 February 1885 when, according to the log-book, "At 16h the note-book for the observation was torn in two and blown away. After 17h no temperature readings were taken, as the lamps could not be kept alight, and the observers could not stand against the wind. At 18h, 19h, and 20h, Mr Omond or Mr Rankin went out at the tower door with a long rope and had to be hauled back. After that the observer did not go out". As with almost all the major storms at the Observatory the wind was from a southerly direction. In 1890 a screen was attached to the wall of the Observatory tower, and this contained thermometers which could be read without going outside in very stormy weather. Under these conditions there was practically no difference between their readings and those in the normal thermometer screens.

A saturated atmosphere was the most usual condition at the summit of the

Inside the observatory.   Horses carrying stores.

Ben and in the warmer months everything outside, including the bulbs of the thermometers, was dripping wet. So, before making a temperature observation, the observer had invariably to remove a film of water or ice from the thermometer bulb. In winter and spring, when the summit was often enveloped in cloud for long periods and the temperature was below freezing point, the supercooled cloud droplets froze on coming into contact with any object on the mountain top. On occasions the resulting deposits of fog crystals (rime) could reach a surprising size. For example on 20 February 1890, after a period with southeasterly winds, it was reported in the Observatory log-book "In afternoon the top of tower was partly cleared of fog crystals; they filled the entire top, except a small portion to the NW, the growths from the three anemometer shafts and the chimney having joined. The crystals on the Robinson anemometer were fully 7 feet long".

Iced-up tower.

The amount of moisture which air can contain as an invisible gas depends on the temperature of the air – warm air can contain much more moisture than cold air. If the temperature falls the air can become saturated, with some of the moisture condensing out as water droplets to form clouds or fog. When a parcel of air rises in the atmosphere its temperature falls and eventually it may reach a level where condensation occurs. Layer-type clouds form where the upward motion is relatively slow over a wide area, and heaped (cumulus) clouds form where individual bubbles of rising air are set off by surface heating. Typically layered clouds are found ahead of and close to the centre of depressions and cumulus clouds in the "unstable" air to their rear. Because of its height the summit of Ben Nevis is frequently above the base of the clouds and so experiences "hill fog" for much of the time. Sometimes it is only the summit area that is "capped" in fog.

23

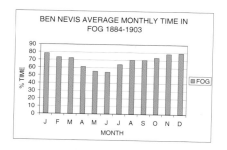

BEN NEVIS AVERAGE MONTHLY TIME IN FOG 1884-1903

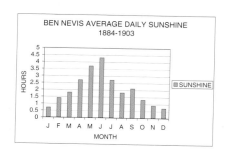

BEN NEVIS AVERAGE DAILY SUNSHINE 1884-1903

The graph showing the observed frequency of hill fog indicates that only from April to July is there a reasonable prospect of having a clear view from the summit, to reward a climber's efforts. During the winter months those who scale the northern cliffs will almost certainly need to be able to navigate safely off the plateau in a whiteout. Except in mid-summer, when there may be some clearance around the middle of the day, there is very little diurnal variation in the fog frequency. Clear conditions at the summit are almost always associated with anticyclones (areas of high pressure) centred over or close to Ben Nevis. As a result of the high frequency of fog, average daily sunshine amounts were low, despite the unobstructed horizon.

It was impossible to keep the anemometer clear of rime for much of the year and consequently instrumental wind observations had to be confined to periods when the temperature remained above freezing point. For the hourly observations the observers estimated the wind direction and force at a position on the flat roof of the Observatory, and calibrated themselves against each other and the anemometer when it was working. The equivalent wind speed for a given force is considerably higher on the Ben Nevis scale than on the well-known Beaufort scale, for example force 8 is 37 knots on the Beaufort scale, but 63 knots on the Ben Nevis scale.

The tower in summer with anemometer, wind vane and lightning conductor.

COMPARISON OF BEN NEVIS
AND BEAUFORT WIND SCALES

	Mean Wind Speed in Knots	
Wind Force	Beaufort Scale	Ben Nevis Scale
0	0	0
1	2	5
2	5	10
3	9	18
4	13	26
5	19	34
6	24	43
7	30	52
8	37	63
9	44	73
10	52	84
11	60	97
12	>64	113

(1 knot = 1.125 miles per hour or 1.854 km per hour)

Reference has already been made to the effects of local topography on the winds observed at the summit of Ben Nevis. Wind roses, showing the percentage winds blowing from the main cardinal points, have been drawn for Ben Nevis (1884-1903) and Cairngorm (1992-2003) (see page 26). The major difference is the very high frequency of northerly observations and low frequency of northwesterlies on Ben Nevis, when compared with the Cairngorm observations. It appears that northwesterly winds are deflected around Carn Dearg and give rise to very gusty northerlies at the summit. These local effects were not appreciated at the time and it was assumed that this major veering of the wind with height was a feature of the air circulation around depressions. Westerly winds were also often lighter than might have been expected at such an exposed site and the strongest winds usually came from the south or southeast with speeds in the most severe storms reaching 120 miles per hour.

The build-up of rime also affected the temperature readings since the louvres of the Stevenson screen could become serrated with rows of teeth which rapidly joined up to form a solid mass, preventing the free flow of air through the screen. A moderate build-up could be chipped away at the time of the hourly

FREQUENCY OF WIND DIRECTIONS

CAIRNGORM 1992-2003   BEN NEVIS 1884-1903

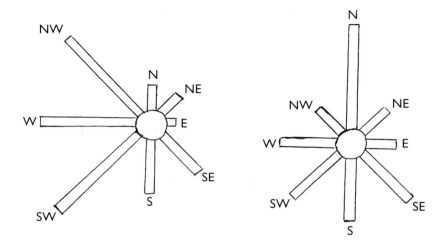

observation but often the only answer was to replace the screen with a fresh one and carry the frozen one indoors to thaw it out. In winter the screens were placed on ladder-like stands and raised as the snow deepened so that they were always kept at the same height above the surface.

Even worse than rime were the not infrequent falls of supercooled rain or drizzle which left a sheet of ice over every exposed surface, including on occasion the observers' faces. This glaze was called by the observers "silver thaw" and on one occasion a deposit of ice about 30 cm deep was left on the summit.

Duplicate snow and raingauges were used, one being taken in each hour to replace the other, its contents being measured at leisure indoors. Despite having a weighted base, on many occasions the gauges were blown out of position, sometimes over the precipice to the north.

Daily weather data from Ben Nevis were published in the Scottish newspapers, which were happy to pay for the cost of the regular telegrams sent to them from the summit, but the Meteorological Office declined the offer of daily telegrams, apparently on the grounds of cost, and asked to be sent telegrams only when conditions of particular interest occurred. Then in 1887 the Meteorological Council stated that occasional telegrams were of no assistance in forecasting the weather (which was hardly surprising) and requested that no further telegrams should be sent. Daily manuscript data sheets of the hourly observations were, however, regularly dispatched to the Meteorological Office in London via the roadman, who acted as mail carrier and nominally climbed the Ben every week, though bad weather in winter could lead to gaps of as much as six weeks between his visits. From the near-pristine appearance of the bound volumes, now held in Edinburgh Meteorological Office archives, it is evident that little, if any, use was made of them at the time.

The daily observation sheet for 13 January 1895 (see next page) shows that it was a day of blizzard conditions with east-southeasterly winds reaching forces 10 to 12 on the Ben Nevis scale. For much of the day the observers could not venture outside to read the thermometers in the screen and readings were obtained from the tower thermometer.

Using a portable Aitken dust counter (see page 51).

Summit shelter in 1995 with severe icing.

Iced-up surfaces after "silver thaw" (freezing rain or drizzle).

BEN NEVIS OBSERVATORY—DAILY OBSERVATIONS.

1895 . Month January Day 13

	Baro. at 32°.	Dry Bulb.	Wet Bulb.	Dew Point.	Elastic Force.	Humidity. Sat.=100.	Visibility. 0 to 5.	EYE OBSERVATIONS. Direction.	Pressure.	ANEMOMETERS. Direction.	Velocity. Revolutions.	Miles.	RAIN, SNOW, &c. Kind.	Amount.	LOWER. Species.	Amount.	Direction.	UPPER. Species.	Amount.	Direction.	SUNSHINE. Hours.	MISCELLANEOUS.
1 Hour,	24·630	20·3			·109	100	0	SE	10 – 11				·0 !		fog							
2 „	4·624	20·3			·109	100	0	SE	9 – 10				0 !		fog						9°	
3 „	4·582	19·9			·107	100	0	SE	10 · 12				0 ?		fog							
4 „	4·547	20·1			·108	100	0	SE	10 · 12				0		fog							
5 „	4·647	20·1			·108	100	0	SE	5 – 9				Sn ?		fog						9.	
6 „	4·603	19·7			·106	100	0	ESE	9 – 10				0		fog						9.	
7 „	4·610	19·0			·103	100	0	ESE	8 – 10				0		fog						–	
8 „	4·541	18·9			·102	100	0	ESE	10 · 12				0 ?		fog						–	
9 „	4·544	18·5	18·5	18·5	·100	100	0	ESE	9 – 11				Sn ?		fog						–	
10 „	4·552	19·0	19·0	19·0	·103	100	0	E	8 – 10				Sn ?		fog						–	
11 „	4·458	19·0	19·0	19·0	·103	100	0	ESE	10 · 12				Sn ?		fog						–	
12 „	4·496	19·1	19·1	19·1	·103	100	0	SE	10 · 12				Sn S		fog						–	
13 „	4·450	19·1	19·1	19·1	·103	100	0	ESE	11 – 12				Sn S		fog							
14 „	4·348	19·0			·103	100	0	SE	11 – 12				0 !		fog						–	
15 „	4·344	18·7			·101	100	0	ESE	10 · 12				0		fog						–	
16 „	4·339	19·0			·103	100	0	ESE	10 · 12				0		fog						9.	
17 „	4·332	19·0			·103	100	0	ESE	11 – 12				0		fog						9.	
18 „	4·451	18·9			·102	100	0	ESE	10 – 11				0		fog							
19 „	4·433	18·8			·102	100	0	ESE	11				0		fog							
20 „	4·483	18·9			·102	100	0	ESE	9 – 11				0		fog						9.	
21 „	4·490	18·9			·102	100	0	ESE	8 · 10				0		fog						9.	
22 „	4·501	18·6	18·7	18·6	·101	100	0	ESE	6 · 9				0		fog						9.	
23 „	4·492	19·1	19·1	19·1	·103	100	0	E	5 – 7				0		fog						9.	
Midnight,	4·495	18·9	18·9	18·9	·102	100	0	E	5 – 7				0		fog						9·0	
Sums,	2·392	48	49	48	·088	00	0		236					·050								
Means,	4·500	19·2	19·2	19·2	·104	100	0		9·8					·002		10						
Max.,	4·647	20·3	20·3	20·3	·109	100	0		11 – 12							10						
Min.,	4·332	18·5	18·5	18·5	·100	100	0		5 – 7							10						

at 21ʰ Min registered —
Barometer jumping heavily

No raingauge out owing to drift
Tower Screen in use from 1ˢ to 8ˢ and from 14ʰ to 21ʰ

R. T. Omond Superintendent.

Daily observation sheet for 13 January 1895.

The Low-Level Observations

One of the chief aims of the Managing Committee was to examine the vertical variations in the physical properties of the atmosphere. Accordingly it had been arranged that the schoolmaster at Fort William should make observations similar to those taken on the summit. These observations were made "five times a day with great punctuality and accuracy" but only at times which did not clash with the duties of the industrious dominie. So, when the organisers of the successful Edinburgh International Exhibition of 1886 presented the Society with £1,000 from its surplus funds, it was decided to build in Fort William a low-level observatory, which would provide continuous records for comparison with those on the summit. The quite orthodox situation of the new observatory was apparently more to the liking of the members of the Meteorological Council, for they proceeded to equip it with autographic instruments which had previously been in use at Armagh Observatory. They also agreed to subsidise its running costs to the extent of £250 per annum, their annual grant to the mountain observatory remaining at £100. Building began in May 1889 and it was hoped to complete it by 15 October, but severe drought had so lowered the level of Loch

Oich that the Caledonian Canal, through which the building stone was to be brought from Elgin, was closed. It was not until July 1890 that the new observatory began to operate fully. "With these observations the changes of the conditions of the weather may be followed hour by hour, particularly those changes so vital and essential to the

The low level observatory in Achintore Road, Fort William.

29

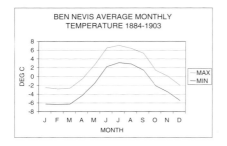

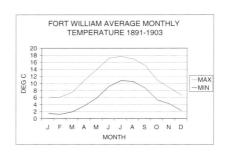

advancement of our knowledge of storms which take place in the lowermost stratum of air between the observatories" was the expressed intention of the Committee.

With the two observatories running in tandem it was possible for studies to be made of the variations with height of different meteorological elements and to see how these varied with time of year and with different weather systems. It was the found that the average fall in temperature between Fort William and the summit of Ben Nevis was 8.5°C, which was equivalent to a change of 6.4°C in 1000 metres. The largest fall was 16.0°C on 19 December 1890, when the summit temperature was -12.8°C and the low-level one 3.2°C. By contrast, during anticyclones the summit temperature could exceed the low-level one (a temperature inversion), often for considerable periods of time, with the strongest inversion being observed on 19 February 1895, when the summit was 9.8°C warmer than Fort William. The lowest temperature observed on Ben Nevis was -17.4°C at 8 a.m. on 6 January 1894. (Much lower temperatures have been observed at inland sites in Scotland on calm, clear nights in winter).

The graphs show the average maximum and minimum temperatures for each month at the Ben Nevis and Fort William Observatories. The annual mean temperature at the summit (for the period 1884-1903) was -0.3°C, while at Fort William (for the period 1891-1903) it was 8.4°C. Temperatures below freezing point have been observed on Ben Nevis in every month of the year and even in the middle of winter temperatures can rise well above freezing point.

The measurement of precipitation on the summit of Ben Nevis was extremely difficult. Much of it fell as snow, which had to be melted in order to obtain the rainfall equivalent, and in strong winds the snow tended to be blown past the gauge rather than into it. Conversely drifting snow could be blown into the gauge even when no snow was falling. It was found that the most practicable method of operation was to exchange raingauges every hour, taking the old one inside the Observatory for the measurements to be made. From July 1890 hourly

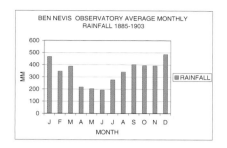

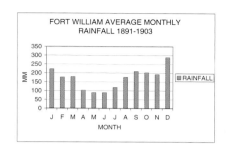

measurements of rainfall at the Low-Level Observatory were obtained from a Beckley self-recording gauge; before that date daily values were available from a Symons 5 inch gauge at the schoolhouse. For mean data the seasonal distribution of rainfall at both sites fitted the pattern generally found in the west of Scotland – high monthly means from September through to March and considerably lower values in April, May and June. However, there was very considerable variation from year to year in the monthly totals. For example in December, which was on average the wettest month in the year, the lowest totals occurred in December 1890, with 95 mm at Ben Nevis and 33 mm at Fort William. By contrast in December 1900 Ben Nevis recorded 1228 mm and Fort William 551 mm.

The high annual rainfall on and among the mountains of western Scotland, by comparison with that recorded in the east of the country is due to "orographic enhancement" of the rainfall, when a moist airstream from the Atlantic meets the mountain barrier inland from the coast and is forced to rise over it. As the air rises it cools and the moisture condenses into clouds, capping the hills. These small cloud droplets may coalesce into much larger raindrops or rain falling from higher levels may sweep them up. As a result the rain is much heavier than that observed at the coast and very high rates of rainfall have been observed, exceeding 12.5 mm (0.5 inches) in an hour. In the warm sectors of depressions heavy rates of rainfall can continue for many hours. (Similar orographic enhancement can occur in the east, when the wind is blowing from the North Sea, but this is of much less frequent occurrence).

Some periods of very heavy rainfall over 24 hours or more were recorded at Ben Nevis and Fort William during the winter half of the year. Almost all of these occurred within the warm sector of depressions, whose centre lay to the north of Scotland. The air in the warm sector had originated over warm tropical seas and even at the summit of the mountain the temperature was above freezing point, leading to a thaw of lying snow at all levels. One of these occasions occurred during 17 and 18 March 1898. The weather maps for 0800 GMT on 17

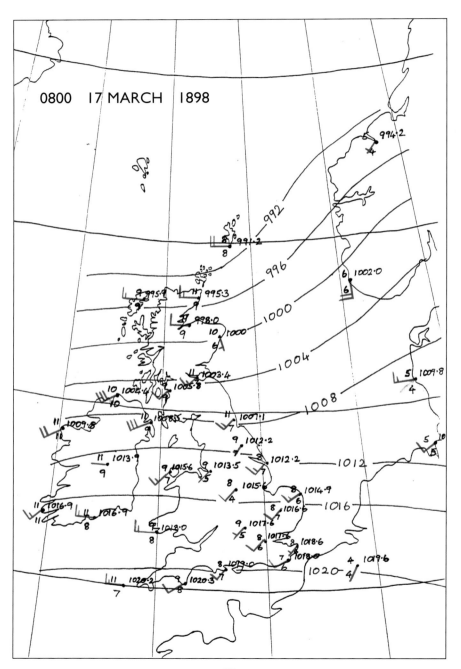

0800   17 MARCH   1898

March and 1800 GMT on 18 March (see next page) show that a warm, moist westerly airstream was covering Scotland and this persisted until the evening of 18 March, when a cold front moved southeast, with the temperature falling rapidly behind it. The graph below shows the hourly air temperature and rainfall measurements at Ben Nevis and Fort William. Heavy rain is defined as a rate of rainfall exceeding 4 mm per hour and it can be seen that at the summit this rate was exceeded for almost all of the time between 3 a.m. on 17 March and 5 p.m. on 18 March.

In the early years of the Ben Nevis Observatory the observers spent ten months of the year at the summit, but after the Low-Level Observatory was opened the duties were rotated between the two Observatories, with staff changing over every three months. A number of volunteers acted as relief observers, including W T Kilgour who wrote the book "Twenty Years on Ben Nevis" and maintained a climatological station in Fort William for a number of years after the Observatories closed. Alexander Drysdale, BSc, acted as a relief observer on a number of occasions, often for a considerable period of time, to enable the regular observers to work at the Society's office in Edinburgh, preparing the data for publication. His set of photographs and lantern slides relating to his work at the Observatory, which he bequeathed to the Ben Nevis collection in the Edinburgh Meteorological Office, together with the notes for a lecture that he gave in the 1930's, provide a vivid glimpse of life at the roof-top of the British Isles.

Ben Nevis & Fort William Observatories 16-18 March 1898

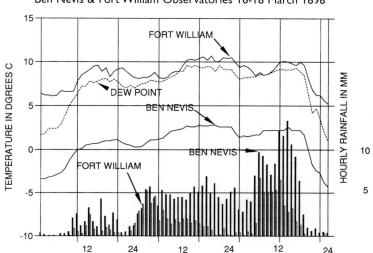

Hourly rainfall and temperature observations on Ben Nevis and at Fort William.

33

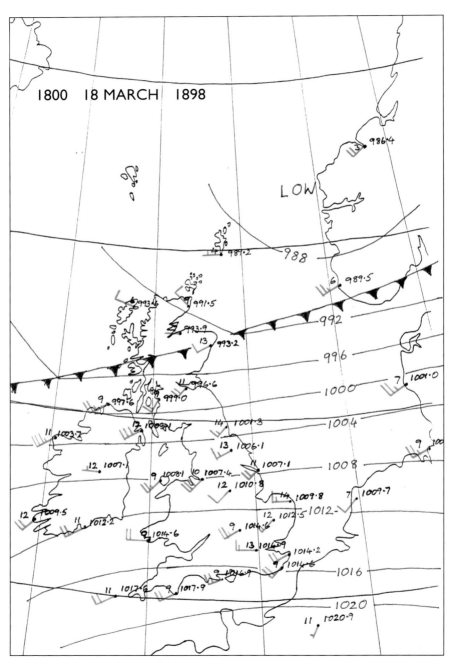

1800 18 MARCH 1898

Life at the Observatory

In the description of the observation routine by Alexander Drysdale it was explained that "for observational purposes the day was divided into watches, two of nine hours and two of three hours each, there being always one observer in charge of the weather. At each hour precisely he read the barometer in the office; then he sallied forth into the outer air where the different thermometers were read, the raingauge changed, cloud and wind notes taken. Various other items were observed at special times, such as depth of snow at a particular post, atmospheric dust, ozone, rainband, duration of sunshine. The hourly observation itself took only five to fifteen minutes, the time depending on the work to be done and the obstacles presented by the weather. Between the observations the observer kept a look out for unusual phenomena – as halos, corona, glories etc, while engaged in the work of correcting and entering up the observations, drawing up daily and monthly averages and discussing points of interest; or in the less severely scientific operations of clothes-mending, tobogganing, snow-shoeing, digging out of doors and windows, or wading through the last-arrived batch of letters and newspapers".

Cornices above Gardyloo Gulley.

During a winter storm the observation routine became much more exciting and hazardous as Drysdale described; "soon the main door, with tunnel and porch, were blocked with drift and the use of the tower door was necessary. The one appalling moment was when the tower door was opened and the 100 mile per hour gale roared past, sucking the air from the building and the heart of the observer nearly from his mouth. Out, nevertheless, onto the roof he went, closing the snow-choked door with difficulty behind him, steadied himself against the gale and waited for a lull to tack over to the guiding rope to the thermometers. The rope attained he slipped his arm around it, and struggled blindly forward, with lantern carefully shielded and head down to escape the pitiless drift. In winter the screen was tied to a stout vertical ladder, up which it was raised step by step as the depth of snow increased. An hour before it was 4 feet above the snow, but now it was overwhelmed by a wreath. The luckless observer had, therefore, to lie down in the blinding drift to read the instruments, and might count himself fortunate if the lantern did not go out at the critical moment necessitating a

DEPTH OF SNOW IN CM AT MID-MONTH
AT BEN NEVIS OBSERVATORY

Year	Oct	Nov	Dec	Jan	Feb	Mar	Apr	May	Jun	Jul
1883/84	nil	102	203	203	267	289	267	305	140	nil
1884/85	nil	nil	84	145	310	310	343	340	221	18
1885/86	79	58	112	137	218	234	310	234	160	nil
1886/87	nil	nil	33	117	99	118	124	129	nil	nil
1887/88	nil	nil	117	117	132	142	155	163	58	nil
1888/89	nil	nil	18	84	118	127	129	nil	nil	nil
1889/90	nil	nil	28	61	168	175	223	178	nil	nil
1890/91	18	56	23	25	97	112	142	91	nil	nil
1891/92	nil	nil	104	132	173	178	145	132	nil	nil
1892/93	58	20	69	66	137	157	140	nil	nil	nil
1893/94	8	53	69	127	239	317	239	244	180	nil
1894/95	nil	89	46	66	84	109	135	15	nil	nil
1895/96	nil	33	84	86	102	132	173	86	nil	nil
1896/97	nil	25	38	84	94	89	127	196	nil	nil
1897/98	nil	nil	61	99	132	178	185	196	56	nil
1898/99	nil	nil	nil	69	127	140	152	119	nil	nil
1899/00	nil	nil	nil	76	145	147	226	142	nil	nil
1900/01	41	48	30	84	112	147	221	129	nil	nil
1901/02	nil	nil	48	102	109	122	150	137	36	nil
1902/03	nil	nil	23	91	109	178	287	307	102	nil

return and a fresh start". If an observer had been blown away in one of the storms the likely entry in the log-book would have been "so and so blown away at (say) 23h. Wind force probably force 12 i.e. 120 miles per hour".

Once snow had built up around the Observatory conditions indoors remained cosy even in the most severe gales and low temperatures. But in late autumn and early winter, before the insulating snow blanket had settled around the building, the observers had to endure rigours so severe that even sleep was impossible. When winds of hurricane force battered the yet unprotected Observatory, indoor temperatures remained well below freezing point and the observers longed for the snow to build up around them. At the onset of the first blizzards, the finely powdered snow penetrated the smallest chinks and settled on the floors of the bedrooms and in the kitchen to within a few feet of the stove. On one occasion a tonne of snow had to be shovelled out from the lobbies and passages.

Snow depths varied considerably over the summit plateau and for consistency observations were made at a fixed post near the Observatory. The table shows the depth of snow observed at mid-month in each year from 1883 to 1903. During October, November and some Decembers snow cover tended to come and go, but thereafter it persisted until late May or June, extending to mid-July in 1885. The maximum snow depth usually occurred in April or May. Snow persisted much longer, often throughout the summer, in the sheltered snow-beds below the cliffs to the north.

In summer the water supply was usually drawn from a tank set up at a natural spring close to the Observatory or from water collected from drainage off the roof but in winter a digging party set out each day to bring in a supply in the form of buckets of snow from the cleanest part of the hill-top. In an emergency they just opened a window and brought in a spadeful.

The natural spring.

37

Bucket drill.

Once the water supply had been replenished the next task was "bucket drill", with the day's accumulated rubbish being heaved over the cliff in an environmentally unfriendly manner at the spot now known to climbers as "Gardyloo Gully". "Bucket drill in winter was not without excitement since overhanging snow and sudden squalls had to be reckoned with. It was customary, therefore, to rope the party to a log fixed under a pile of stones. Luckily no-one ever slipped over".

During the winter part of the year there were very few visitors to the Observatory, but in summer the summit could be thronged with "tourists" who had taken advantage of the pony track, for whose use they were expected to pay a toll of one shilling. Further revenue could be obtained from the charge made to tourists for sending a telegram to their friends, and the Post Office at Fort William supplied a boy to handle these. Such visitors were considered a very mixed blessing, especially as many of them could not be convinced that it was a meteorological and not an astronomical observatory and that there were no "telescopes and things" to be seen. The ultimate insult came when some of the visitors insisted on tipping the observers on departing!

An enterprising Fort William hotelier set up a "hotel", where simple lodging could be had for the night and refreshments obtained. This was open only during the summer and the few winter visitors, including some from the Scottish Mountaineering Club, were made welcome at the Observatory.

It is not surprising that the observers took great delight in recording the fauna of the summit; no doubt the flora would have been observed too, had there been any. Snow buntings were the only other permanent residents besides the observers, whom they never ceased to charm with their low melodious warbling. One became an Observatory pet, coming to the window for food. The croak of ravens was often heard but the birds rarely seen.

A family of stoats usually took up winter quarters about the hotel or the Observatory stable and they were often seen in their white coats with black-tipped ears peering in at the windows. Mountain hares were quite frequently seen slightly further down the mountain and one young hare, which had been caught near the Lochan, was added to the staff. It soon became quite tame and developed strange tastes "including a liking for cinders and scientific literature". Another pet features in the log-book entry for 20 February 1904, which has a note of tragedy. "During the last few days the Observatory cat has been suffering a form of paralysis. Today, it was destroyed. It was brought to the summit as a kitten a few months old on 26 July, 1895".

Time does not appear to have hung heavily on the observers. In summer they played a game of rope-quoits on the lead roof and in winter the principal recreation was tobogganing. The course began near the Observatory and proceeded by a series of moderate descents for about a kilometre, ending on a little knoll beyond the Plateau of Storms, just before the continuous steep descent of the Ben. There was a latitude of 20 to 30 metres on either side of the course before they were in danger from the northern cliffs or the southern slopes. Certain landmarks provided important guidance as to whether they were on course and if not rapid abandonment of the sledge was called for. On one occasion a tobogganeer rigged a sail on his sledge and only just missed accompanying his craft over the precipice.

Tobogganing off the roof of the Observatory building.

From left to right: A. Rankin, R.T. Omond and R.C. Mossman.

The Log Book

The Observatory log-books are fascinating documents, with their accounts of the experiences of the observers, the comings and goings of staff and visitors. They also contain detailed descriptions of haloes, glories, aurorae, St Elmo's fire, Zodiacal light and so on (many of them illustrated with meticulously drawn diagrams). The early ones are particularly full of interesting details and include valuable indexes to their contents.

The eerie experience of the electrical discharge called St Elmo's fire was so common as to be accepted as almost a normal occurrence, but on occasions it was so spectacular as to deserve a special mention. On October 29 1887 it was recorded that "at 1h 5m St Elmo's fire was seen in jets 3 to 4 inches long on every point on top of the tower and on the top of the kitchen chimney. Owing to the number of jets on each cup of the anemometer, this instrument was quite ablaze. On the kitchen chimney the jets on top of the cowl were vertical, and those on the lower edge of the same horizontal. The fizzing noise from the different places was very distinct. While standing on the office roof watching the display, the observer felt an electric sensation at his temples, and the second assistant observed that his (the observer's) hair was glowing. On raising the snow-axe a little above his head a jet 2 to 3 inches long shot out at the top. A shower of snow and snow-hail (conical) was falling at the time, and the wind was a variable S to SW breeze".

Fortunately thunderstorms were quite rare events at the Observatory since they could have very alarming and dangerous consequences, despite the presence of a lightning conductor on the tower. On 19 June 1895 clicks were heard on the telegraph apparatus – a not unusual occurrence – and heavy hail which later turned to snow was falling. "The two observers were dining in the hotel and Mr Kay, who was indisposed, was sitting in the office and noted the earth currents. No thunder was heard or lightning seen till 14h 57½m, when the observer on duty was leaving the hotel. It was then that a great flash filled the hotel, accompanied by a terrific crash. In the Observatory there was an even more vivid flash and more deafening report. The telegraph instrument emitted a cloud of

1887 -

Edmay 15 Bright light seen to N^d though heaks in
fog at 1ᵏ — possibly auroral —
a few passing glories seen at 14ʰ.10ᵐ
Solar Corona observed on passing scud at 12ʰ
always double sometimes triple = best seen when
scud was uniform in thickness — not fibry —
and thin enough to see the blue sky through .

Radius of Inner Red 3°.35' 3°.31' { 3°.52' 3°.21' { 4°.13'
        outer Red   4°.28 5°.43 { 6°.55'   { 7°.38

" The bracketted values were taken at as nearly as possible
the same time —

At 9ʰ.20ᵐ the fog-crystals on
T stand for Hygrometer were
measured . Next the wood
was one inch deep of white
badly defined and rather
powdery crystals = then 3/4
inch of brown well defined
feathery crystals = then 1/10 inch
of pure white crystals, grown
in the last half hour . Between the 3/4 layer and
the 1/10 inch layer was a belt of minute black
specks which had apparently formed while

Extract from the log book with descriptions of a corona and deposits of polluted rime.

smoke, and also the stove and stove pipe. The office was suffocatingly filled with smoke. In the kitchen a large flour tin, a smaller box, and a small picture in the vicinity of the lightning protector were hurled across the room. Parts of the telegraph instrument, the plates of the protectors, and in many places the wires were fused... After the barometer observation at 15h, the observer having forgotten the raingauge returned for it, and only then noticed smoke and flame issuing from behind the wainscot between the kitchen and the office doors. Messrs Miller and McDougall and two visitors, on being summoned, were almost immediately on the scene to assist, and the fire was quickly overcome". This was the worst of a number of such occurrences, but damage was never serious and no one was injured. It is recorded that one "cook left on the day after a thunderstorm", but cooks appear to have come and gone at quite a high frequency.

The Observatory was in operation during a period when there was much heavy industry in the Central Lowlands of Scotland, and when the air reaching Ben Nevis came from that direction it was often heavily polluted. As a result the ice-crystals which were deposited from fog were often of a brownish colour, contrasting with the snowy-white crystals observed when much cleaner air came from the west or north. On 23 December 1884, with west southwesterly winds, "To-day the feathery snow crystals, forming on exposed surfaces, were grey-brown in colour", but on 24 December, when the wind had swung into the north, "The snow crystals forming today are white in colour, and contrast strongly with those of yesterday".

Since foggy weather could be described as the norm on Ben Nevis, occasions when the top was clear of fog receive a considerable amount of attention in the log-book. Spells of more than twenty-four hours of clear weather were most likely to occur in May and June and least likely in December and January and were

Looking south-southeast with banded cloud trapped below an inversion.

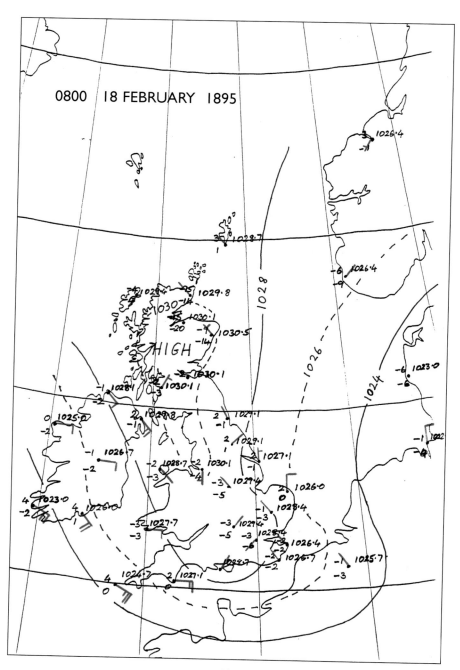

0800 18 FEBRUARY 1895

associated with high pressure systems over Scotland. On these occasions the air was often extremely dry, though the valleys below could be filled with damp, murky cloud through which only the higher peaks emerged into the sunlight. On 15 January 1888 the log-book recounts "Summit clear all day. From 1h till 6h the aurora was faintly visible. Fog in valleys all day to the height of about 2500 feet. In afternoon glimpses of the lower hills and moors were got through breaks in the fog and it was observed that the Moor of Rannoch was white with hoar frost, as were also the hills to S and NE of Ben, but these only to a height of about 2500

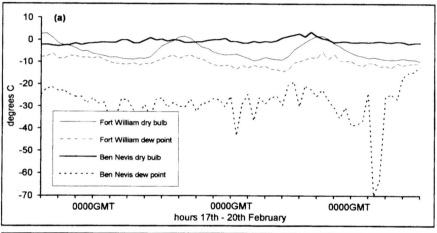

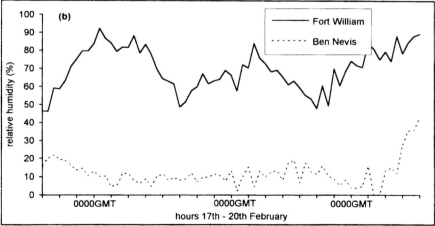

(a) Air and dew point temperatures (°C), and (b) relative humidities (percentages) at Fort William and Ben Nevis for February 1895.

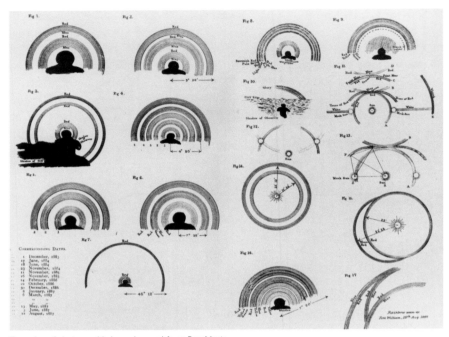

Examples of glories and haloes observed from Ben Nevis.

feet, all above this having no hoar frost". The temperature at the summit during the morning was around 5°C and the relative humidity below 20% while at Fort William the temperature was around 1°C, and relative humidity about 88%.

In an anticyclone (region of high pressure) air is slowly sinking from higher levels in the atmosphere and it warms as it does so, leading to a fall in the relative humidity. If, as happened quite frequently, the lower boundary of the sinking air was between the Ben Nevis Observatory and the Fort William Observatory, then a temperature inversion (rise of temperature with height) was observed (see pages 44 and 45). A notable example of this occurred from 17 to 20 February 1895, when an anticyclone lay directly over Scotland. The graphs show the hourly air temperature and relative humidity at the two sites. At the summit there was little diurnal change in temperature and the relative humidity remained below 20% from 1800 GMT on 17 February until 0600 GMT on 20 February. For several hours during that period it was less than 10%. At Fort William the temperature showed a regular diurnal cycle, rising above freezing point in the early afternoon and falling to about -9 degrees C by morning, with the afternoon relative humidity only falling to about 50%.

Low cloud can become trapped below an inversion, leading to "anticyclonic gloom", while above the inversion the fortunate hill-walker enjoys brilliant sunshine and a view of mountain summits emerging from a sea of cloud.

When they could see the sky the observers had a grandstand view of the many optical phenomena going on around them, with strikingly coloured glories, corona and haloes around the sun and moon, the shadow of Ben Nevis above Mull in the morning and above the Eastern Highlands in the evening. Careful measurements were made of angles and radii, but there is no doubt that they also appreciated the beauty of what they saw. There was almost a note of disappointment when a lunar corona was only a double one instead of having three or four rings or a solar halo did not have a full accompaniment of mock suns, arcs of contact etc.

During the summer months from 1885 onwards there were notes in the log-book recording the appearance in the northern sky of "pearly cirrus" – often in the form of "ribbed cirrocumulus" – and some photographs were taken. There is no doubt that these were the rare noctilucent clouds, which occur at a height of about 80 km, and are visible against the twilight sky, remaining illuminated by the sun while the lower clouds are in darkness.

There were many detailed accounts of aurora, which was seen on as many as 38 nights during 1892 near sunspot maximum and only once in 1900 at sunspot minimum.

Accounts of unusual visibility when the magnificent panorama of mountains, glens and islands was disclosed to the observer must have tantalized the many visitors who climbed the mountain only to find that they had "missed the view but viewed the mist". On a few occasions the Hills of Antrim in Ireland, almost 200 km away, were visible through a telescope between the Paps of Jura.

Looking southeast with fog trapped below an inversion.

R T Omond, first Superintendent from 1883 to 1895, at the door of the Fort William observatory.

Personalities

The man who planned and himself minutely analysed the Ben Nevis observations was the permanent Secretary and presiding genius of the Scottish Meteorological Society, Alexander Buchan. He was appointed to that position in December 1860, and became one of the leading meteorologists of the nineteenth century. He was also a distinguished member of the London Meteorological Council, a position that to a man of his friendly nature must have been delicate and difficult in the prevailing friction between his Society and the Council. His first paper on "The Meteorology of Ben Nevis" appeared in 1884 in the Journal of the Society and dealt with the observations of Wragge and his assistants. Many more publications on the subject were to follow until his death in 1907.

Alexander Buchan, permanent Secretary of the Scottish Meteorological Society from 1860 to 1907.

Robert Traill Omond served as Superintendent from the opening of the Observatory until 1895, when ill-health made it impossible for him to withstand the rigours of life there. He continued, however, in overall charge of the work from the Society's rooms in Edinburgh. Angus Rankin, who, with James Miller, worked at the Observatory throughout its period of operation, eventually took over as Superintendent. After the opening of the Low Level Observatory the number of permanent observing staff was increased to four, and there was no lack of volunteers to relieve them when this was required.

One of these, Alexander Drysdale, has already been mentioned, and another was R C Mossman. Mossman had been educated for a business career but his early interest in weather observing was encouraged by Alexander Buchan and in 1889, at the age of nineteen, he was allowed to act as a relief observer on Ben

R C Mossman in his study, 1906.

Nevis. He was back there again in 1890 and 1891. Like the rest of the staff he learnt his meteorology "on the job" and he then went on to become a noted climatologist, publishing in 1896, 1897 and 1902 his monumental work on "The Climate of Edinburgh". He joined the Scottish Antarctic expedition in 1902 on the "Scotia" and found his Ben Nevis experience stood him in good stead when making meteorological observations in polar regions. The leader of that expedition, W S Bruce, also gained experience of meteorological observation in an arctic environment during his periods of service at the observatories in 1895 and 1896. The "Scotia" overwintered at Laurie Island in the South Orkneys in 1903 and a shore-based meteorological station was set up there. The hut, which provided the living quarters, was named "Omond House". In 1904 three Argentinians were brought to Laurie Island on the "Scotia" to take over the running of the meteorological site, with Mossman staying on for the first winter, and observations have continued there until the present day, making this the longest continuous meteorological record in the Antarctic region.

Being a fully-equipped mountain laboratory, the Observatory was frequently visited by scientists wishing to conduct experiments requiring the special conditions provided at its height of 1344 metres above MSL. In July 1885 Professor Vernon Harcourt and an assistant performed experiments on the intensity of light from flames at low pressure.

Hygrometric studies were carried out by H N Dickson in 1885/6 and A J

Omond House, Scotia Bay, South Orkneys with joint Scottish-Argentinian staff 1904 (copyright RSGS).

Herbertson in 1892 to 1894 to test the validity of Glaisher's tables, which were used at that time in the UK to calculate the dew-point, relative humidity and vapour pressure from readings of the dry and wet bulb thermometers in a Stevenson screen. The very wide range of relative humidity which occurred at the summit and the lower pressure provided an ideal opportunity for experimenting under a wide range of conditions. Their results showed that tables based on Regnault's formulae (now universally used) were much more reliable than Glaisher's. (The

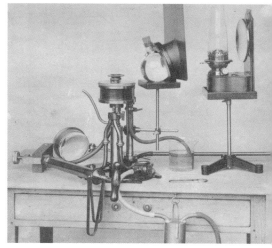

Aitken dust counter.

humidity data on the observation sheets sent to the Meteorological Office in London were computed from the Glaisher tables, but corrected values can be calculated from the original dry and wet bulb temperatures and the pressure readings).

Another set of experiments which was carried out at the Observatory was organised by John Aitken of Falkirk, using two versions of his dust counter. The large version was set up in the tower and a small portable model used when the wind was carrying smoke from the chimney towards the tower. Between 1890 and 1894 a considerable number of experiments were carried out. On some occasions when the wind was from a northwesterly direction there were no dust particles in a given sample of air, but the highest reading of 14,400 particles per cc occurred on 11 April 1891, when there was a fresh wind from the southeast. The log-book that day reported "Summit clear from 11h till 19h, fog during the rest of the day. The fog crystals were brown all forenoon. While the top was clear the dust in the air was deposited on the fog crystals, tipping them all jet black. Very thick haze all round all the time the summit was clear".

One of the young students who acted as relief observers during the summer months was C T R Wilson, who later invented the Wilson cloud chamber and who was awarded a Nobel Prize for physics in 1927. In 1955 he recounted how his interest in glories and corona was aroused during a short period of duty at the Observatory in September 1894 and the following spring he started making laboratory experiments on clouds formed by the expansion of moist air. He

C.T.R.Wilson,
Nobel prize-winner for physics in 1927.

W.S.Bruce, leader of the "Scotia" expedition to
the Antarctic in 1902-1904 (copyright RSGS).

found that if Aitken nuclei (dust particles) were present, then small expansions caused large numbers of small droplets to be formed, but if these nuclei were removed a considerable degree of supersaturation could be obtained without condensation occurring. Under these condition an ionizing particle (such as an α-particle or β-particle from a radio-active source) would ionize the molecules in its path and these in turn acted as condensation nuclei leaving a trail of droplets and a visible track. The Wilson cloud chamber became one of the most important tools used in atomic physics research.

Financial Difficulties

Despite the very low cost of construction of the Observatory and bridle path, the remarkable response of the Scottish people to the appeal for funds and the fact that the staff received modest salaries, (the Superintendent only received £100 per year and his assistants around half of that) the Management Committee was continually faced with money problems. Men had to be employed to keep the path in order and the Observatory supplied with stores and material. Horses alone were an expensive item; the cost of repairs to harness and of replacing horses indicates the strenuous nature of the work of haulage. The Post Office levied an annual fee of £357 for the rental of the telegraph cable. The total expenditure to June 1885 was about £6,000; the deficit was then a mere £600, but the Directors could hardly expect the liberality of subscribers to continue at its initial level. A toll of 1s from each person using the path to walk up the mountain and of 3s from each "climber" on horseback and the profits from the sale of a guide book brought in on average £50 per annum. (Either the number of climbers was then very much smaller than at present or many must have by-passed the half-way house near the lochan where the charge was levied). The Press Association paid about £100 a year for cabled weather reports, while the annual grant from the Meteorological Council remained at £100 for the high-level and £250 for the low-level Observatory.

The Observatory accounts were kept separate and distinct from the ordinary funds of the Society but there regularly appeared in the Society's accounts entries denoting loans to the Observatory Funds of £300. Continued subscriptions from the Scottish people, a gift of £150 from the British Association in 1893 and, in 1896, a minor windfall of £1,875 from the trustees of the estate of the Earl of Moray temporarily relieved the anxieties of the Directors. But in 1898 came the first mention of imminent closure, a circumstance that, in the words of Sir John Murray of the "Challenger" could be avoided only if some rich patriotic Scotsman gave a cheque for £500 to tide them over for one year. By next morning's post the required cheque came in from an enthusiastic amateur meteorologist, Mr Mackay Bernard (of Bernard's ales), and he provided similar sums in the next three years. These, with further donations of £600 from anonymous donors barely covered the running expenses, which were now £1000 per annum. Appeals were being continually made to the Treasury, but in vain.

Then in 1902 the Meteorological Council informed the Society that they would withdraw the grants of £350 at the end of that year. This came as a bolt from the blue and the Directors issued a Memorandum explaining the financial situation and stating that unless something was done they would have no option but to close the Observatories. There was a public outcry in Scotland, questions were asked in Parliament and a Treasury Committee of Enquiry was set up to look into the administration of the annual grant of £15,300 to the Meteorological Council. In the meantime sufficient funds were obtained to keep the Observatories going until the Committee was due to report in 1904.

The case which the Directors made to the Committee was that the Observatories had proved their value in relation to scientific research and that they had considerable potential as an aid to forecasting, that they were a national asset whose upkeep should be fully supported from government funds and that if such support were not forthcoming they would have to be closed. Support from the Meteorological Office was lukewarm at best. They stated that they had not found the Ben Nevis observations to be of any value in forecasting. The response from the Directors was that they had not even tried to use them! By

Summit ruins in winter.

Summit ruins in summer with remains of Wragge's cage for the thermometer screen.

Wragge's cage in 1882.

contrast in April 1904 the German Meteorological Office, Deutsche Seewarte, asked for daily telegrams containing information which was to be used in preparation of their forecasts and later comments indicated that they at least had found them to be of considerable value.

When the Treasury Committee finally reported they only recommended that the annual grant of £350 should continue, and their statement gave the impression that (deliberately or otherwise) they had paid little heed to the evidence given to them by the Scottish Meteorological Society that the sum required was about £950 per annum. The Directors issued a Memorandum explaining the situation in which they said "It is to the Directors a matter of profound disappointment that in this wealthy country it should have been found impossible to obtain the comparatively small sum required to carry on a work of great scientific value and interest, and that they are now obliged to dispose of the Observatory buildings and dismiss the staff".

The last entry in the log for 1 October 1904 differs from all others by being formal and terse. "This forenoon the barometer stood at about 25 inches. The temperature ranged from 30 to 33. The wind was W to NW, blowing about 10 miles an hour. Snow was falling, and mist enveloped the summit. By command of the directors, the observations were discontinued at the Observatory after the noon readings were recorded". A week later, after dismantling and supervising the removal of equipment, the staff barricaded and locked up the Observatory and descended the mountain.

The building and bridle path were handed over to the Proprietors of the ground in accordance with the stipulation of the feu charter and the Fort William Observatory was advertised for sale. The total cost of building, equipping and maintaining the Observatories during the twenty-one years from 1883 to 1904 was just over £30,000 of which less than one-sixth was contributed by the state.

On 21 June 2000 the John Muir Trust purchased the Ben Nevis Estate, which included the summit area with the Observatory ruins, from Duncan Cameron Fairfax-Lucy. Ben Nevis had been owned by his family since 1834. The John Muir Trust began detailed monitoring work on the condition of the ruins and have pledged to ensure that they are protected from further serious decay.

Postscript

The data from the Ben Nevis and Fort William Observatories were published in full, together with extracts from the log-books and a number of papers analysing the observations, in the Transactions of the Royal Society of Edinburgh, Vols. 34, 42, 43 and 44 parts I and II. Volume 43 also contains summary tables of monthly totals and averages for each of the years throughout the operation of the two Observatories. Many papers were published at the time by Buchan, Omond, Rankin, Mossman, Herbertson, Aitken and others on various aspects of the meteorology of Ben Nevis, but these have often been forgotten or ignored by those who lament the paucity of mountain weather data in Scotland. There is much that could still be learnt from them.

Buchan died in harness in 1907, at the age of 77, still working hard on a study of the interrelations of barometric pressure, temperature, humidity, rainfall, cloud, sunshine and wind at the two Observatories and Omond ably supervised the publication of the last two volumes.

Even as late as 1909 the Scottish Society was "still burdened with considerable financial obligation on account the Ben Nevis Observatory" and an appeal was made to members for assistance. Such was the response that the debt was cleared within a few months. Up until the 1914-18 war many still held the hope that it would be possible to reopen the Observatory, but after the war shrinkage in the membership of the Scottish Society, among other things, led to its amalgamation with the Royal Meteorological Society in 1921. In 1920 the Meteorological Office had taken over the responsibility for organising and running the climatological network in Scotland.

The subject of the reopening of the Observatory has been raised from time to time, and there has been no lack of volunteers to resume observations, but the cost has always been considered to be prohibitive. One of the principal original aims was to provide, in the days before the invention of radio, early warning of the approach of Atlantic storms, but this is now much more easily achieved by other means. What has changed since the beginning of the twentieth century is the degree of interest in mountain weather per se. Climbing and hill-walking take an increasing number of people onto the mountains at all seasons of the year and providers of mountain weather forecasts require actual observations to assist them in the preparation of the forecasts. Major downhill skiing developments in Scotland have required planning data for their development and current weather data and forecasts for the safe running of their operations in the skiing season. Electricity power lines and pylons, radio and television masts

Carn Mor Dearg and Ben Nevis from Aonach Mor summit.

have been (or are planned to be) erected at quite high levels in the UK, in some cases on the actual summits of mountains, where they are affected by both severe icing and high wind speeds. The modern solution to these demands for high level weather data has been to design automatic weather stations which can operate in such severe environments.

In 1971 the deaths from exposure of six young people hill-walking on the Cairngorm plateau led to an examination of the need for improved forecasting of mountain weather and the development by Heriot-Watt University Physics Department of an automatic weather station which was capable of operating on the summit of Cairngorm (1245 metres) throughout the year. This site had a small stone-built hut with a mains power supply, housing relay equipment for mountain rescue co-ordination. The ingenious solution which was devised to cope with the problem of severe icing was to house the instruments in a heated

Rime on Aonach Mor automatic weather station.

58

insulated container and only expose them to the elements for a short period of time to make the actual readings. Readings are made twice in every hour of temperature, wind speed and direction averaged over 2½ minutes, and maximum 3-second gust during that 2½ minute period. Measurements with the improved Mark II model started in March 1977. As might be expected there were interruptions in the records, some of which unfortunately coincided with periods of particular interest weatherwise, such as January 1984, but considering the conditions experienced the equipment has worked extremely well.

An automatic weather station for use in severe environments and which also requires mains power, has been designed by the Meteorological Office and trials with this were carried out outside the Ptarmigan restaurant on Cairngorm in the late 1980's. Operational versions of this automatic weather station were set up on Cairngorm and Aonach Mor (near Fort William) in 1990 and on the Cairnwell at Glenshee ski area in 1993. Although these automatic stations cannot provide the full range of observations that were possible with a manned mountain observatory, their development and use would have gladdened the hearts of the old observers.

Observatory in winter with Wragge's cage and stands for the thermometer screens.

Sunset from the observatory ruins.

The Future

What is the future of the Ben Nevis Observatory ruins? In 2002 the Nevis Partnership, a charitable company limited by guarantee, was set up to implement a management strategy for an area comprising Glen Nevis, Ben Nevis and the surrounding mountains and slopes (the catchments of the River Nevis and the Allt a' Mhuilinn). Section C1 b (Ben Nevis summit, high plateau and Coire Leis management) of the Nevis Strategy, the working document which serves as a blueprint for the management plan, refers specifically to the longer-term management of the Ben Nevis Observatory ruins and states:

"Consolidation of the Observatory ruins and removal of non-essential cairns, memorials (except peace cairn) and other artefacts. Interpretation of the Observatory and a simple collective memorial may be provided off the mountain, possibly in Glen Nevis".

Working in close association with the John Muir Trust (landowner of the summit area) and Alcan Smelting and Power UK (landowner of the lower slopes and approaches) the Nevis Partnership will seek to consolidate the ruins, using only the techniques that were used in the 1800's, to secure the above stated aims and objectives. In addition the Nevis Partnership will seek to provide educational and interpretive opportunities for all groups interested in the invaluable work undertaken by the early weathermen of Ben Nevis.

The members of the Nevis Partnership are the Highland Council, Scottish Natural Heritage, Fort William Community Council, Sport Scotland, Glen Nevis Residents Association, John Muir Trust, Lochaber Mountain Access Group, Inverlochy and Torlundy Community Council, Mountaineering Council of Scotland, Alcan Highland Estates, and Glen Nevis Estate. Forestry Commission Scotland and the Highlands of Scotland Tourist board are associate members.

Details of the management plan can be found at **www.nevispartnership.co.uk.**